Questions that triggers purposeful actions.

4 Questions of WHY?

A guide to a lasting purposeful life.

BALQEES HAMZAT

DEDICATION

To every Young, Optimistic and Unique mind whose purpose is meant to SHIFT the world.

WHY?

I knew I wanted to do anything creative from the day I could articulate what a future is, there was a BUT... My mum wanted a medical doctor and this was how the journey to medicals began.

This seems like the story of many amongst us but even the lucky few can't articulate that thing they are passionate about because everything is just as blurry as what will happen the next minute.

At 7 you wanted to be a doctor, at 11 a lawyer, and at 17 rushing to get into the university and at 20 many are trying to find their footing in whatever space they find their selves.

Ranging from parents to friends and everyone we are privileged to meet, we all have been asked different questions over time about our purpose in life in the simple yet heavy context "what do you want to be in the future?"

I must say this itself is very annoying as if you aren't feeling bad enough that you can't articulate all of the things you want out of life yet saying "I don't know yet" is another war because everyone asking start to perceive you as being unserious, sometimes useless and not passionate about anything.

Then these people will tell you to find a purpose for your life or even outrightly foster you with ambition with the saying ***"you will get to like it".***

 When people tell me to look for passion and purpose, I am like "this thing does not drop from heaven" so where will I find it?

Our curiosity that was stolen from childhood made us forget **purpose** sits deep within us waiting for us to take out time to search for it in quietude away from a noisy world.
 Passion comes from having a purpose which is the reason for YOU and I being in the arena called LIFE.

The discussion today is all about find the Clarity of WHY...

What is your WHY?

My favorite author Robin Sharma calls WHY that thing that keeps you up at night, wakes you up early in the morning and makes you feel fulfilled just knowing you are a part of it or it is a part of you.

So ask yourself WHY
- Are you in that relationship?
- Working very hard to earn as much as you can?
- Trying to learn this much to become all you could be?
- Take on so much responsibility?
- Are you going this far to develop yourself to the fullest?

WHY DO YOU DO ALL YOU DO?

Begin to ask yourself these questions, you must have your list of why's because
"If your why is powerful the how will be easy."

According to Balqees Hamzat in 2020, WHY is an acronym for ***What Hunt You.***

It is a nagging, hollow but deep feeling within us, it is a calling we haven't answered and it wouldn't be silenced by mere worldly materials but that thing we were meant to become and do.

There is something that HUNTS every one of YOU.
 YOU to me mean YOUNG, OPTIMISTIC & UNIQUE which is the reason things strike us differently.

I began finding WHY in 300l, I wasn't enjoying medical school but the relevant discussion is what I can do for a year nonstop as well as writing and reading self HELP books.

 I had to create a balance because I needed to graduate but then the calm wasn't coming if I do not write in a day or produce a podcast in a week.
All this became my solace, I could express myself and I found reading what I wrote or listening to myself interesting. It came with a sense of fulfillment.

Solace, joy, and fulfillment are what your purpose gives you and when you haven't found your purpose, that deep calm even during hard times can't be there. This is how it feels for everyone but about different spheres.

Think of that thing that brings you calmness and happiness when doing them...***Start thinking.***

ROOT OF YOUR WHY...

Like we already discussed, WHY is the purpose, a reason for existence that ***YOU can be unapologetic about*** and this is rooted in the meaning you want your life to GIVE and HAVE.

Everyone as something they want to be known for, that thing they can lay their life for, mine is living productively because I am sure ***a great life comes from living each day greatly.***
Everything I do is centered on this, from writing to podcasting and who will be in my circle.

Now ask yourself that one thing you want to be known for.

For instance, on my tour in the country called Instagram, I walked into one of the roadside shops and the lady in charge had it boldly written on her that she wants to be the ***most sort after host in the world***.

All I could see is how achieving the above is what will give her life meaning, it is what wakes her up daily, keeps her up at night and the only thing she would have that would make her feel fulfilled while going to bed at night.

Chadwick Boseman wanted to stand in front of God and tell God he used all of his talents and he brought nothing back which is why he made himself a force to reckon with in every movie he starred in.

 *What is that thing that does all of the above **to and for YOU**?*
Once you know what it is then you've found your purpose or should I call it YOUR WHY?

Not finding one's WHY is the cause of many staying in stressful jobs, relationships, and all that do not serve them.

Being clear on your WHY will let you know the difference between Passion and stress because *passion is working hard on what you believe in* and Stress *is working hard on what you do not believe in* according to *Simon Sinek the WHY guru.*

This lockdown served many a dish they should either eat cold or heat up.
What did you do with your dish?

Many are *complaining, binge-watching, and trying to escape* a life that is already a reality and this I call *living like a VICTIM*

How are you living your life?
What is YOUR destination on this road called Life?
What is your vision? With no vision, humans will wither away.
What is your mission? Without a mission you are nothing.
What are your dreams? For a dreamless soul will perish.

Sit down today, close your eyes, visualize what your perfect day will look like, the kind of health, wealth, power, and influence you will possess, after few minutes your mind will begin showing you something else, this is the envision stage, your mind begin to create a clearer picture, putting a name to the image you have seen.

 Then get a pen and book, write all you saw in your mini dream, then ask yourself why you want to have all of those.

I asked you to visualize your day because a great life is a pile-up of days lived greatly.

Now let me ask you... **WHY NOT?**

Immediately you get your pen and write out your dream, vision, and mission, your ego kicks in, that little annoying voice that tells you all you can be and cannot be without letting you try. This is ***the stay safe do not grow zone*** of life.
Many living the life you aim for do not fall into this trap of the EGO because ***they take risks so they can learn and grow as they go.***

WHY NOT?

- Why not see how much you can grow into the person you envision just by sitting and taking time to clarify your WHY.
- WHY NOT take the risk for all the joy doing those things your heart long for would bring?
- WHY NOT see how much you can learn by developing a growth mindset?
- WHY NOT understand you cannot put a number on the people your one decision to take control of your life can Influence?
- WHY NOT for the people your purpose can take out of poverty and helplessness silence the voice of your Ego?

Your WHY is what bridges the gap between the life you want and the life you currently live.

Chadwick Boseman spent the last four years of his life creating a monument of himself in the heart of every living soul, WHY NOT DO THE SAME?

Here is one secret we all know but do not heed to "You all do not have a choice than to live till death is ready for you, so ***why not see how much and how far you can go in the amount of time you have left?***"

Here are three steps to finding your WHY.

☐ Know your WHO

This is all about who you are, your core values, what you can die for, and what you will always stand for.

The above will become the rock you stand on when the world keeps sinking in the quicksand of ***perceived awesomeness,*** it will become that thing you are unapologetic about.

I do not want to associate with anyone not willing to grow, you like complaining and not finding solutions you can't be in my circle, you do not say the positive thing we can't relate to.

I have a standard and this is what allows anyone in or out and yes you can call it pride or what you like, but it is me.

I will say this to those wanting to belong to every circle they can find "whatever you stand for make sure your friends are in line" so you won't digress. This will serve you every time and every day of your life.

⬜ Link your WHO to your WHY.

A secret many do not know… Your WHY (purpose) comes mostly from your pain.

That thing we won't want another individual to suffer from.
That thing you won't want your kids to experience. Sometimes they are moments you cannot tell another soul.

Once we can go through this phase and come out victorious, we tend to find joy in helping others pass through it.

But this should not take you away from your core values but it should only help you key into growing better and bigger every time you walk another soul through *this valley of the unknown into the light they are meant to see.*

 Once you have these two sorted next is **HOW**

☐ HOW WILL YOU CREATE VALUE FOR OTHERS TO TAP FROM?

This is when you begin to give. The hallmark of human existence is being able to share your knowledge, being able to help people leave the dark corner you once were.

John Obidi calls this growing horizontally not vertically. In the human-made world called the INTERNET, there is access to information that can transform your life or that you can use to transform that of other people but the main problem is aiming for fame and wealth when you have no value to bring to the table.

You aren't clear on who you are, what you stand for, why you want the things you want, and how you will go about getting what you out of life but your eye is on the fame and name you can gather.

O wrong now, you aren't doing well at all.

 Learn to fall in love with HOW you do what you do not what you get from it.

Every day on my status, I enjoy just sharing my knowledge and letting people access what I have accessed Be a part of my joy

Stop looking for passion when you do not love your process, *in your process lays your passion*.

The passion is felt from how you discuss the details of what you do, how you morph each process to fit the other, what stresses you and how you finally moved past it and how the success and failures reward your soul because of the lessons you've learned.

Another secret from my bag of secrets: *It is only shallow people that talk about what they get from what they do and not how they do it.*

 When you meet new people, talk about how you do what you do so they can buy into your idea. *Once you love the process, the success or failure, in the end, becomes a lesson to learn from and a stepping stone to greater things.*

So I was asked a question that does it happen that what one is passionate about might not be meant for someone? Putting it better "what if one isn't good at what he's passionate about"?

With my brain lighting up, I remembered this thing is ***mindset related***.

To me, there is nothing called *not being good enough but it is possible to* **not be willing to be good enough**.

Not willing to be good enough is when you are not willing to change from fixed to the growth mindset, to learn, grow, get a mentor or coach, pay for courses, and ready to learn without permission.

 I once wrote something in one of my blog post that *"Once you are willing to learn, you will surpass those with the talent"*

Consistency and persistence will always be rewarded above talent any day and we all have to pay a price to live our dream in reality.

This price is consistency and resilience to pushing one's self toward that dream and goal even when giving up seems like the best option.
read the post here.

But if you don't mind "my I know it all spirit", I can assure you there is a little voice in your head speaking right now like, ***this isn't meant for you, you can't do all of what she is writing, you cannot even get it right***, now I tell you to ask that voice this little question **WHY NOT YOU?**

Simply reply to all it blabbing with **WHY NOT ME?**

This voice must give you a very concrete and solid reason WHY you cannot have the life you wish for but should be contented living in the realm of mediocrity all your life. Let me give the voice a name, it is called EGO.

Ego is a very lazy and annoying spirit in humans that does ***"I too know"*** even when it knows nothing, it seeks validation at every point and when not given destroys your thought process so you can feel unworthy.

I wish EGO was human so I can spank the nonsense questions he spews out of him.

Kindly connect me to EGO so I can ask it... **WHY NOT YOU?**

Let me remind EGO that YOU
- Have the brains
- Can make decisions
- Can study the plan
- Can put in the work

Needed to change your life, grow to the fullest of your potential, to make your dreams come true so you and your family can be so healthy, powerful, and financially safe that nothing can get through.

Do not think I am done with your EGO, I am not, and I am staying around to shut it up forever so you and I can walk together through the journey of your ascent to greatness.

Just like humans, our EGO is resilient, now that it has no answer to WHY it can't be YOU it is saying something else, calm down please let listen…

EGO just said it's not yet time for all of that. Can you imagine the audacity?

Sweet little EGO wanting to run the course of your life just said it's not time to be great, stable, financially safe, healthy, happy, joyful, and purposeful.

EGO said it is not time to live the life you were meant to live, give meaning to your life, and for your life to become a source of hope, joy, and influence to others.

This time I will ask EGO a question without your permission

…WHY NOT NOW?

I need to remind you that there never was and there never would be a better time to take the controlling power of your life back from whatever you gave it to.

Have you forgotten you are created **uniquely** so you can thrive and Influence others to do the same?

Your ego is reminding you of what happened the last time you aimed for changes that will lead to greatness in your life. So what? You have failed to realize that EVERY ROADBLOCK IS MEANT TO PREPARE YOU FOR THE OBSTACLE IN YOUR NEXT LEVEL OF SUCCESS.

It is not about what happened to you in your past, it is about how you reacted to it, <u>your reaction is all that make every situation into a lesson to be blessed from or a lesson to regret over time.</u>

I am handing you a new sheet to re-write it all, I am handing you my fresh eye to see the things you have seen differently, I am dusting the lights so your mind can become clearer to the opportunity in every obstacle you face.

I am here longing for you to shut the voice of your ego but listen to **the voice of your inner wisdom that calls you great when the world calls you nothing, the voice that wraps you in its warmth in the cold island of life.**
It is that voice that is the most worthy of your time and attention.

That voice is calling you to begin doing things differently with every circumstance handed to you.
Everything you've been handed by life was meant to serve you, they are meant to help you grow into that human that would astonish the world, ALLOW THEM.

Do not try to change the sea, the soil, or the arrangement of the seasons but let its obstacles serve you, problems teach you and pressure become a privilege for YOU.

SITUATION	COMFORTABLE OPTION	UNCOMFORTABLE OPTION
Free time	Play video games, check the Facebook feed, chat on WhatsApp, troll on Twitter, watch Instagram videos and reels.	Read a book, take a course, listen to a podcast, re-check your goals, create plans for the next day.
Thank God It Friday	Go to the club, check out the new bar in your area, hang out with the guys (for married people).	Spend the night eating dinner with the kids, take wifey out for dinner, Spend time with your family.
Bed Time Do's	• Think about the bad things that happened during the day then move to complete that unfinished movie series	• Think about the good things that happened during the day, write them down then move to sleep so you can go to bed with the joy of a day well spent.

	so you can feel better. • Chat all through the night and wake up late.	• You get to wake up early feeling fresh and good.
Morning Routine	Wake up, pick up your phone, check your mails, and scroll through your social media for the gist you missed the night before.	• Wake up at 5 am • Workout for 20 minutes (skipping, jumping jacks, burpees, planks). • Pray, meditate, and journal. • Spend at least 20 minutes reading a book, taking a course, or listening to self-help audios.

The table above depicts situations in our daily life that can either be improved to increase our productivity or left alone so we keep operating in the cult of average.

The comfortable option depicts what 95% of humans in of those situations will pick but the 5% ruling the global space that we all look up to will pick the uncomfortable option because they understand that *living a life that will matter involves picking the hard over the easy.*

The change you want in your life will only come when you have become that change on your inside, change your attitude to the events in your life, change your language to yourself, change your personality to mirror who you want to become, change the way you communicate with your kids, spouse, family, and co-workers.

Tap into your ability to be whoever you want as long as you're willing to work for it because we most times attract what we put our energy into.

Learn to work harder on yourself than on your job.
WHY?
Working on your job will make you a living but
working on yourself will make you a fortune.

~ Anonymous

ABOUT THE AUTHOR

Balqees Hamzat is an alumnus of the University of Ilorin with a degree in physiology and years of activism for good communication, health, and personal growth as an undergraduate and beyond.

She is a strong believer in the ability of young minds to perform with values and compete at a world-class standard which is why she created SHIFTAIN (Serving Humanity by Influencing Future Thrivers An Inch) where she holds live discussions every Thursdays.

She is a productive growth advocate and a volunteer in organizations aimed at providing youths with lessons on living a value-filled and relevant life.

Her favorite pass time is producing podcasts and writing on the little things done daily that amount to a life well-lived.

She aims to connect with amazing young minds from all walks of life if that person is you;

Connect with Balqees through:

Her Blog

Instagram

Twitter

Telegram

Anchor

JOIN SHIFTAIN